THE AMAZON ETHNOBOTANICAL GARDEN

CONSTANTINE ISSIGHOS

Copyright 2013 © Constantine Issighos. Published in Canada. Printed in U.S.A. No part of this book may be reproduced or transmitted in any form or by any means, electronic or mechanical, including photocopying, recording, and/or by any information storage and retrieval system except by a reviewer who may quote brief passages in a review to be printed in a magazine, newspaper, or on the web without written permission in writing from the author/publisher. For information, please contact www.awaqkunabooks.com

NorthWater is an imprint of Awaqkuna Books Inc.

Vol. 20 Of THE AMAZON EXPLORATION SERIES:
AMAZON BOTANICAL GARDEN

Library and Archives Canada

ISBN ISBN 978-0-9878601-9-4

Library and Archives Canada Cataloguing in Publication

ATTENTION CHILDRENS ASSOCIATIONS, BOOK STORES, PUBLIC OR PRIVATE LIBRARIES: quantity discounts are available on bulk purchases of this book series.

THE AMAZON EXPLORATION SERIES
Children's Books
by
Constantine Issighos

1. Upper Amazon Voyage by River Boat
2. The People of the River
3. The Children of the River
4. Amazon's Nature of Things
5. Echoes of Nature: a Beautiful Wild Habitat
6. The Amazon Rainforest
7. Amazonian Sisterhood
8. Amazon River Wolves
9. Amazonian Landscapes and Sunsets
10. Amazonian Canopy: the Roof of the World's Rainforest
11. Amazonian Tribes: a World of Difference
12. Birds and Butterflies of the Amazon
13. The Great Wonders of the Amazon
14. The Jaguar People
15. The Fresh Water Giants
16. The Call of the Shamans
17. Indigenous Families: Life in Harmony with Nature
18. Amazon in Peril
19. Giant Tarantulas and Centipes
20. Amazon Ethnobotanical Garden
21. Amazon Tribal Warrios

The Amazon rainforest is full of diverse plants and trees known to have beneficial medicinal properties. The number of potentially useful medicinal plants growing in the world's largest rainforest is estimated to be in the thousands. Mankind would certainly benefit from the further application of these Amazonian plants. It is estimated that 120 drugs currently manufactured by western pharmaceutical companies are directly derived from Amazonian botanical sources.

The indigenous peoples of the Amazon rainforest have long utilized proven medicinal methods. These methods have been passed from generation to generation in accordance with diverse tribal spiritual and social customs. The indigenous conserve, use, cultivate, manage and exchange botanical knowledge as a fundamental component of their Amazonian lifestyle. Their botanical experiences are made up of a whole set of knowledge systems, ecological practices and socio-cultural dynamics that shape their approach to healthcare. Within the indigenous context of biodiversity, in their ecological, epistemic and cultural domain, their environment provides food security, healthcare and spiritual balance. In their cosmos, botanical gardens are simultaneously wild and cultivated, conserved and shared, sacred and manipulated, food source and cultural script. Botanical genetic diversity is thus connected to ecological, medicinal and cultural values. For example, each one of the varieties of the medicinal plant Ginger (Zingiber officinate) is a food source as well as serving as a particular kind of pain relief. In the case of Huanduc (Brugmansia suavealeu), some varieties of this medicinal plant are used in liquid, while others are applied on the injured skin. The diverse varieties of Nettle (Urera caracasava) have differing medicinal powers and are used according to the intensity of the bodily pain. The popular Hierva Luisa (Gymbopogon cirtatus) is served as a tea and is also used in ritual ceremonies. The Ayahuasca plant (Banisteriopsis caapi) is strictly used by Shaman in the ceremonial spiritual catharsis of a person's troubled psyche.

 In these indigenous tribes there is a regular gathering of genuine Shamans (spiritual-healers) and Curanderos (traditional-healers) who share and preserve their indigenous cultural heritage. The traditional-healers and shamans of the Amazon are part of an ancient tradition that has been working with remarkable medicinal plants for thousands of years. Both healers' ancient traditions are shaped by the beliefs that the natural world and its spiritual energy are a unified force, that nature (matter) creates everything and that it is sacred. They believe that their fate and the survival and perpetuation of all living things are inescapably linked to the well-being of the environment. For more information on the role of the Shamans and traditional-healers you may want to read The Call of the Shaman, in the The Amazon Exploration Series.

Part of the remaining article includes botanical remedies from the Upper Amazon rainforest of Peru, a region in which I have spent a considerable amount of time. This is the area that is currently of most interest to North Americans and Europeans. It must be noted, however, that although there are literally thousands of potential medicinal plants that could be add to the world's pharmacopoeia, there are but a few that have reached that status. Several of the following botanical remedies are well known and commercially available. You and your family may have heard of some of them, either in natural or extracted form. There are also some remedies that large drug companies do not want you to know about because such knowledge infringes on their trade secrets and thus on their profits.

BOLDO (Pneumus boldus)

This medicinal plant is found in Chile and Peru. Boldo leaves are boiled to extract its medicinal properties. The brew is used by indigenous people to treat liver ailments and gallstones. It is recommended by European scientists as a diuretic, laxative and liver tonic. Boldo comes to North America via German and other manufacturers. It is not commonly found in non-specialized health-food stores; it may be ordered online via reputable companies.

CAT'S CLAW (Uncaria tomentosa)

This medicinal plant is also known as "Una de Gato" due to its curved stem structure that resembles a cat's claw. This is the most recent rainforest medicinal plant to emerge in commercially available quantities. It hails from the Peruvian rainforest. The indigenous Ashanikas tribe along the Peruvian/Brazilian border is known to have used this medicinal plant for thousands of years. Hence, there is the well-known trade-name "Ashanikas Una de Gato." There is large-scale scientific research being done to demonstrate its considerable immunostimulant action.

This plant was "discovered" in 1974 by the Austrian scientist Klaus Kiplinger while talking to an indigenous healer. His initial experiments with Cat's Claw showed positive results. Available research is encouraging in the area of cardiovascular treatment. It should be noted that there are 13 known species of Cat's Claw, but only 3 contain considerable medicinal properties. Purchase this medicinal plant in its natural form and from a reputable supplier. Strenuous efforts by the Peruvian government have been implemented to prevent endangering supplies, a common problem with other medicinal plants, such as Suma and Lupacho herbs.

COCA LEAVES (Erythoxylum coca)

I do not hesitate to list a plant that has a dubious reputation and which, as a source of cocaine, is not legally imported into North America and Europe. At peril of sounding like an amateur proponent of coca, I must declare to you that "Coca leaves are not cocaine" in the same way that "Grapes are not alcohol." For more information on the extensive use of coca leaf flavour in popular products around the world, including in Peru and Bolivia, you can read my book "For God, Country and Drug Prohibition" available from Amazon.com

The indigenous of the oxygen-thin Andean highlands of Peru and Bolivia chew coca leaves on a regular basis, thus inducing energy and relieving fatigue, hunger and thirst. Chewing coca leaves is not drug addictive, although the leaves may affect your gums after prolonged usage.

CINCHONA (Cinchona species)

The entire modern era of ethno-botany research began in the mid-1800s by navigator-merchants who were looking to market medicinal herbs that cured malaria. Catholic monks of South America were known to carry with them a small bag containing Cinchona bark and used it to treat sailors and explorers whose suffering from the disease. The plant contains the only source of natural quinine, the original malaria remedy. Botanical science eventually synthesized quinine, but it is still possible to obtain cinchona bark and use it as an immunostimulant. It has anti-viral and anti-pyretic properties that treat headaches, leg cramps and colds.

COMMON NASTURTIUM (Tropaeolum majus)

In the Upper Amazon of Peru, this plant is commonly used to heal flesh wounds. It is commercially exploited as an important antibiotic, one of the few that comes from a higher quality of medicinal plant species. It has a great safety record since patients do not develop resistance, addiction or allergies to it.

SUMA (Pffafia particulate)

From the Amazon rainforest of Brazil, this plant was introduced to the North American herbalist market in the early 1990s. The plant Suma is also known as "Para Toda" which means "for everything" in Portuguese, thus giving some clue as to what benefits might be expected from its use. The indigenous people of Brazil use it as an aphrodisiac, tonic, energizer, anti-cancer aid, immune enhancer and diabetic remedy.

LAPACHO (Tabebuia avellandedae or Tabebuia impetiginosa)
This medicinal plant is also commonly known as Pau D'arco. This is perhaps the best known Amazonian herbal remedy available in North America. It has been recommended for many ailments, including Leukemia, and to relieve the pain of chemotherapy and arthritis. It demonstrates anti-oxidant effects and is an inhibitor of bacteria, viruses, parasites and fungi. It is considered one of the world's great tonic herbs.

PHYLLOMEDUSA BICOLOR
Strokes, seizure, depression and Alzheimer's disease are extreme conditions and illnesses that an aging population around the world faces. These illnesses are treated by natural plant remedies as well as by the secretions of an Amazonian frog called Phyllomedusa bicolour.
An extract from the skin of this giant tree frog is widely used by the Matses indigenous tribe of Peru.

THE FUTURE
The list of effective natural remedies is very long and beyond the scope of this book. There are some serious questions however, regarding the availability of natural herbs to cure illness. Who should do it? Drug companies? Herb companies? Government agencies? What about the indigenous people? How do we protect the environment from overharvesting?
Currently, multinational drug companies are rushing to the Amazon rainforest in search of novel medicinal compounds. Following them are a great number of herbalists whose motives are not entirely clear. Some are tempted to follow modern advertized gimmicks and the promise of a utopian life.
To my readers, I say this: our primary task is to respect and preserve all aspects of indigenous culture and the ancient botanical knowledge of the precious rainforest, including the plants and animals, while simultaneously finding ways to benefit from the Amazon's ethno-botanical garden which contains most of the earth's healing agents.

Constantine Issighos   The Amazon Exploration Series

THE AMAZON ETHNOBOTANICAL GARDEN

The Amazon Exploration Series — Constantine Issighos

THE AMAZON ETHNOBOTANICAL GARDEN — 10

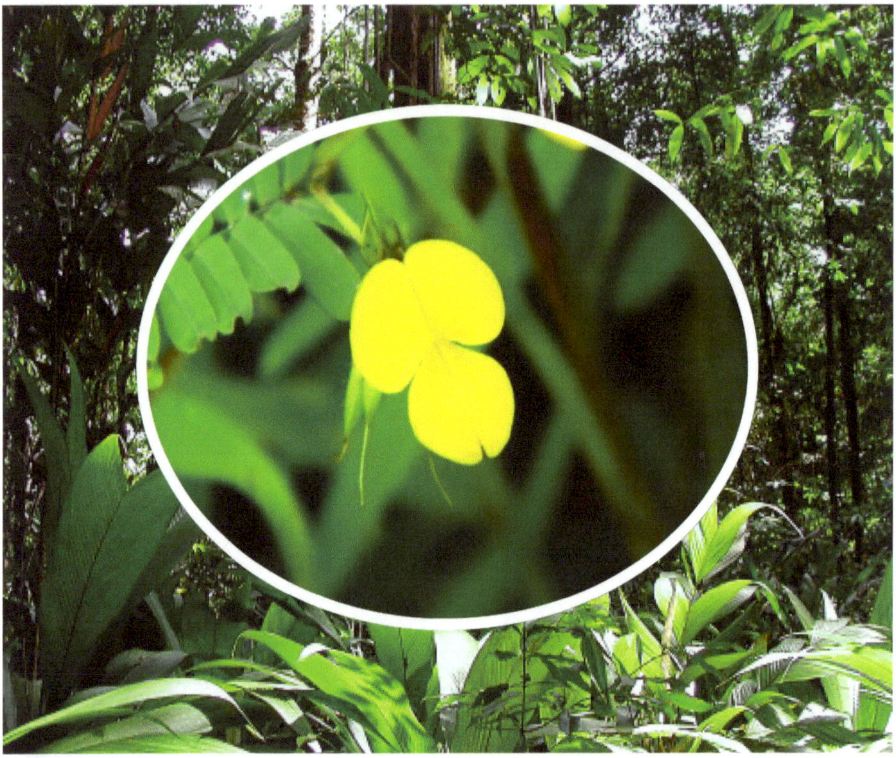

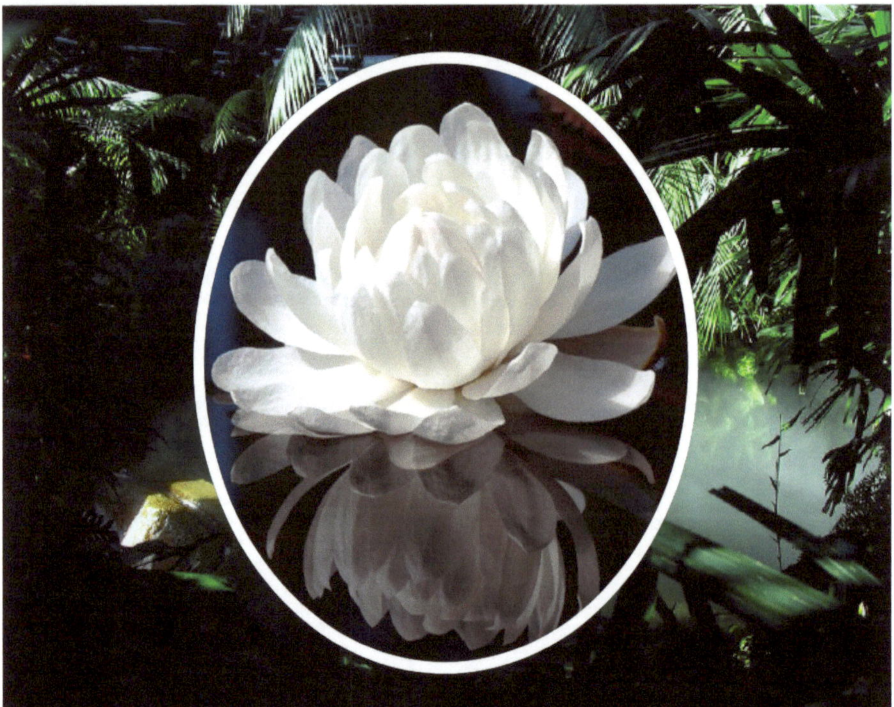

Constantine Issighos   The Amazon Exploration Series

THE AMAZON ETHNOBOTANICAL GARDEN

Constantine Issighos   The Amazon Exploration Series

THE AMAZON ETHNOBOTANICAL GARDEN

Constantine Issighos The Amazon Exploration Series

THE AMAZON ETHNOBOTANICAL GARDEN

The Amazon Exploration Series   Constantine Issighos

THE AMAZON ETHNOBOTANICAL GARDEN   18

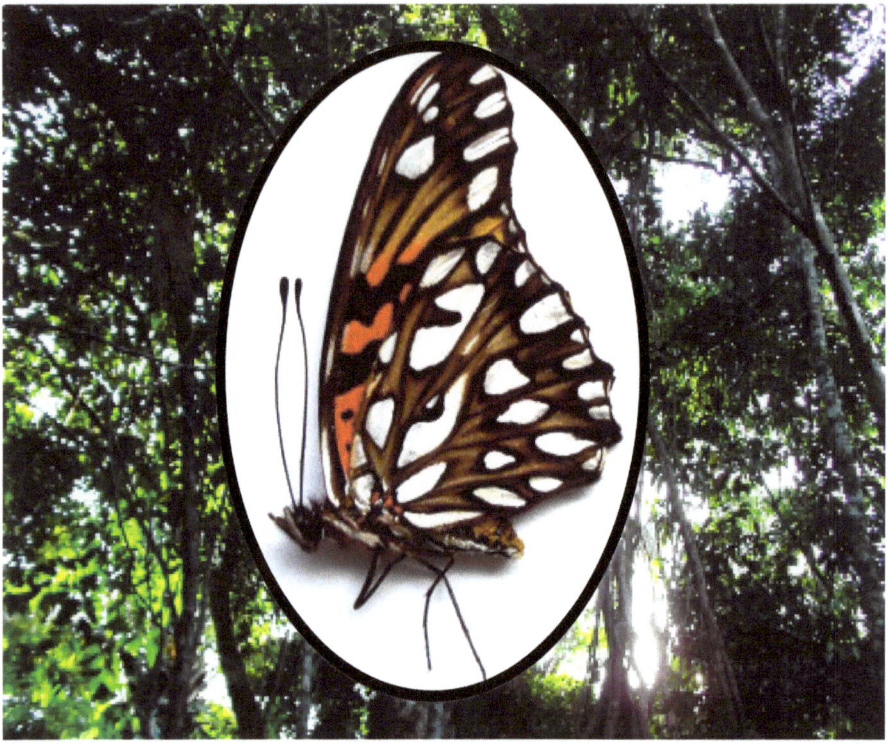

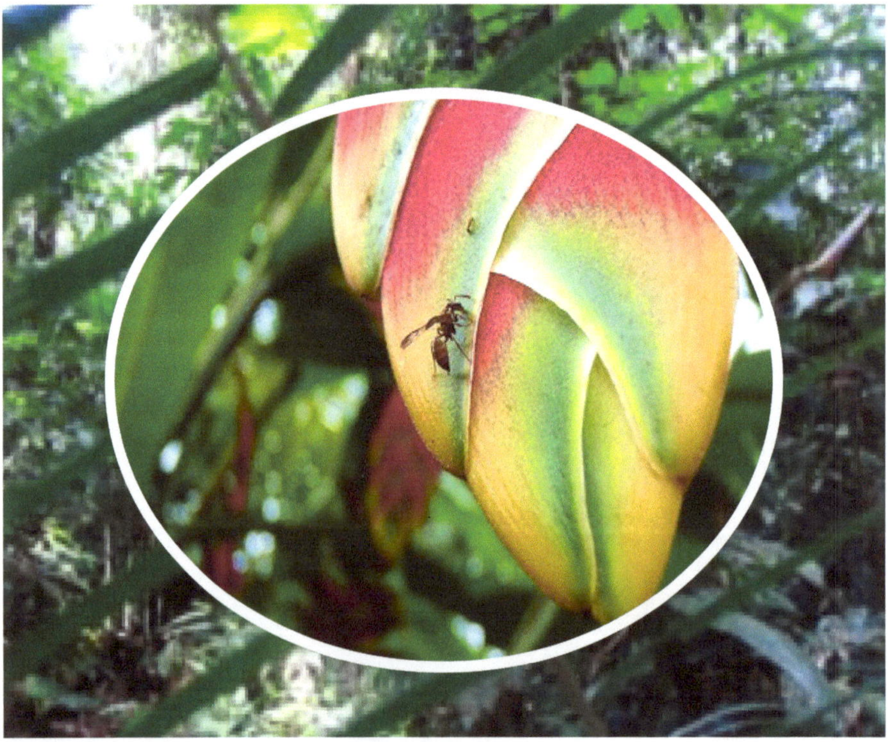

The Amazon Exploration Series   Constantine Issighos

THE AMAZON ETHNOBOTANICAL GARDEN

The Amazon Exploration Series — Constantine Issighos

THE AMAZON ETHNOBOTANICAL GARDEN

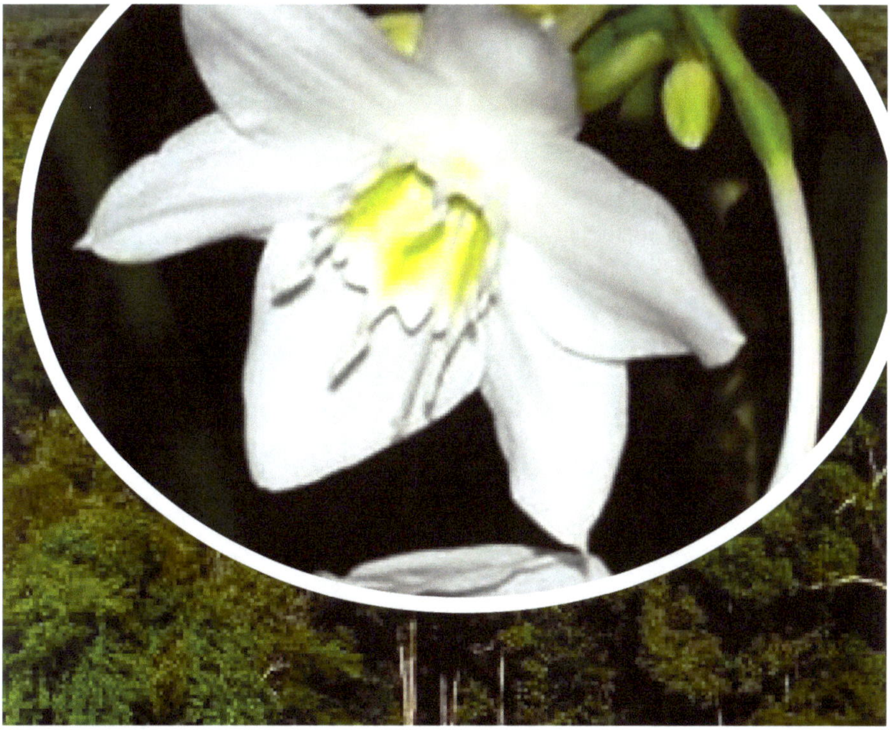

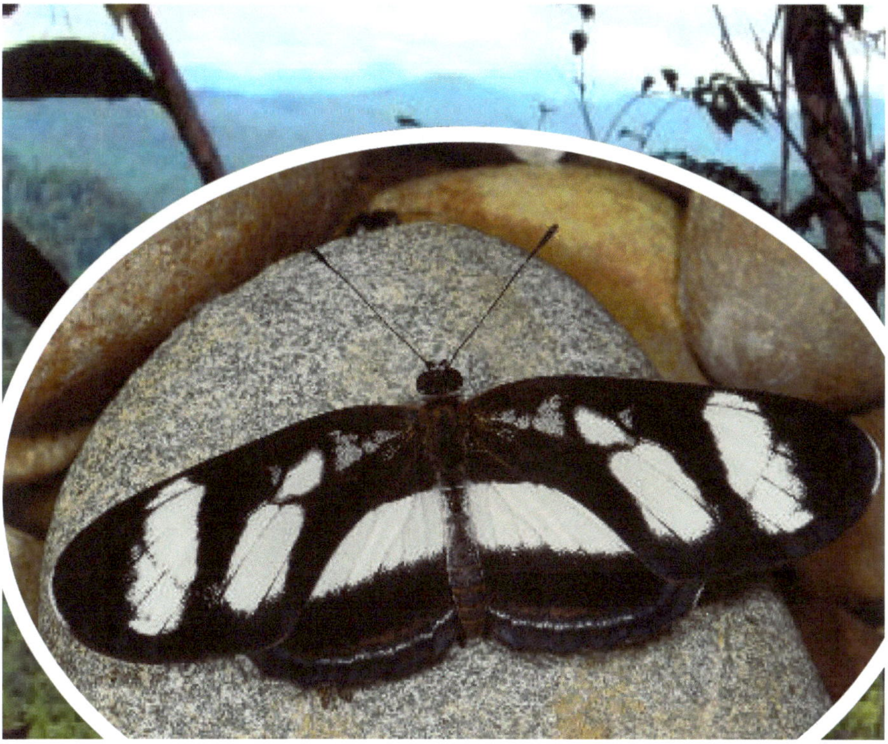

The Amazon Exploration Series — Constantine Issighos

THE AMAZON ETHNOBOTANICAL GARDEN

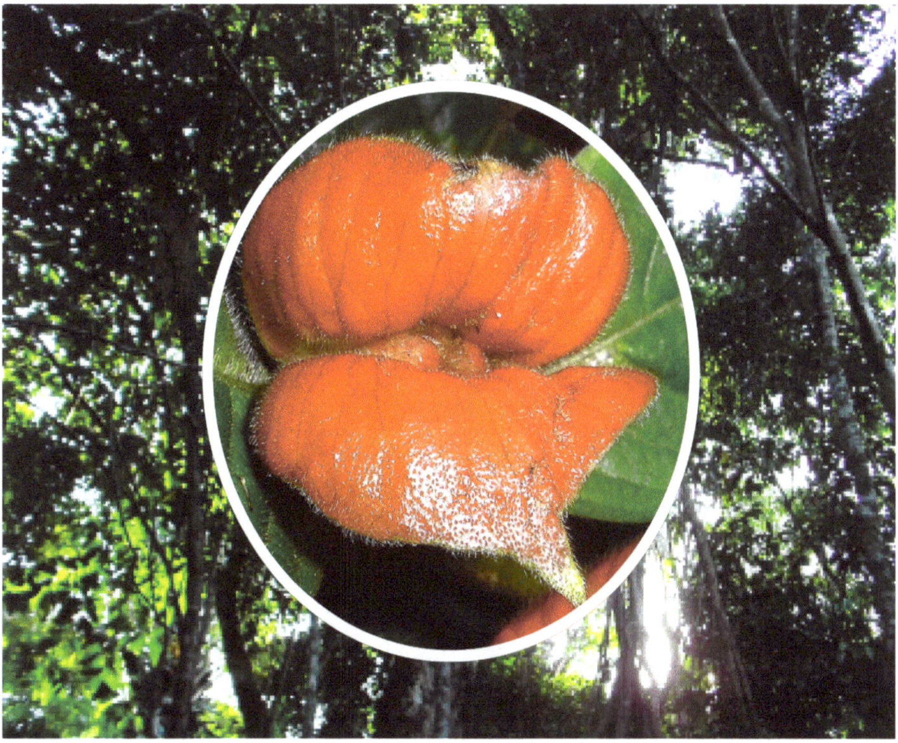

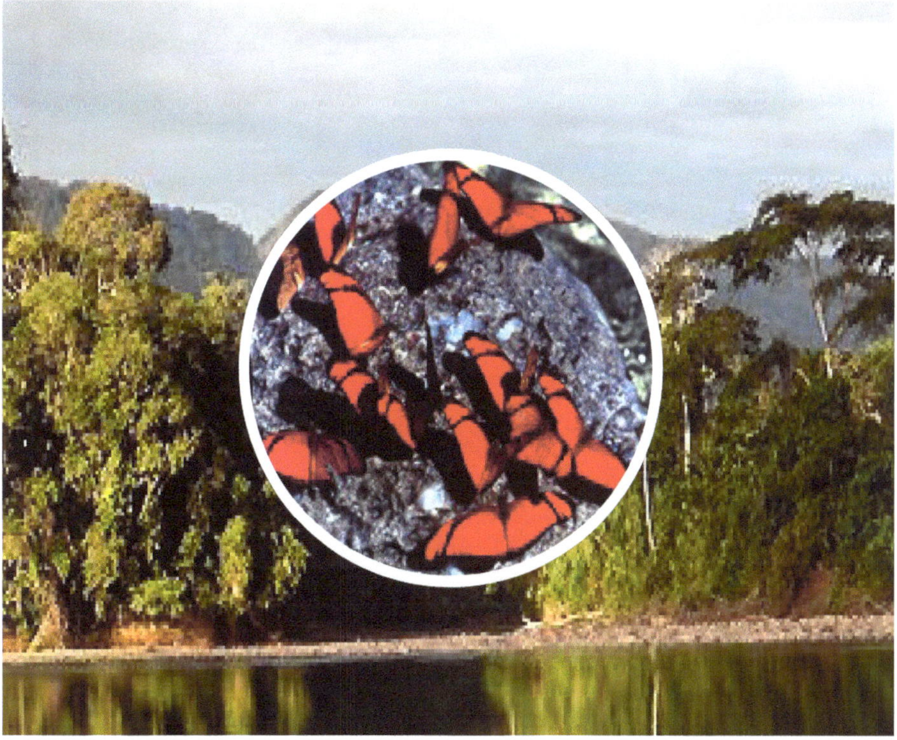

Constantine Issighos   The Amazon Exploration Series

THE AMAZON ETHNOBOTANICAL GARDEN

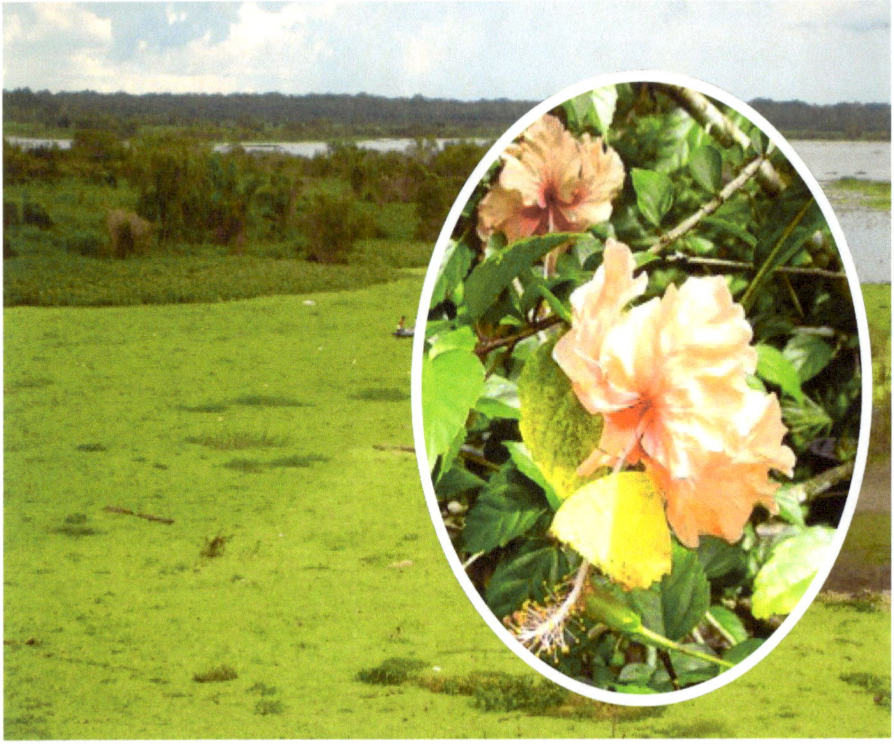

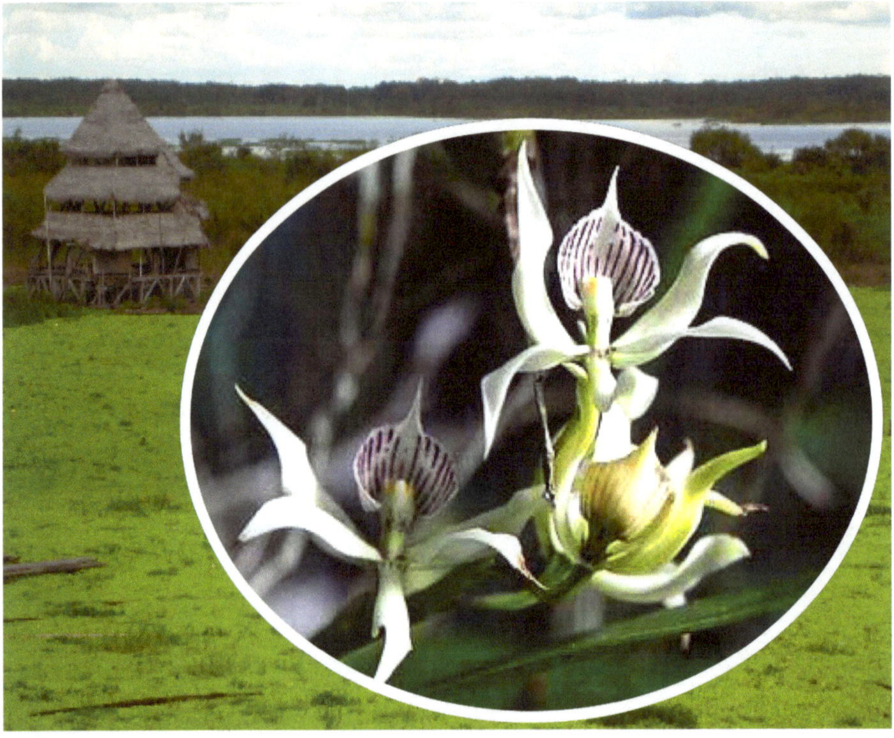

THE AMAZON ETHNOBOTANICAL GARDEN

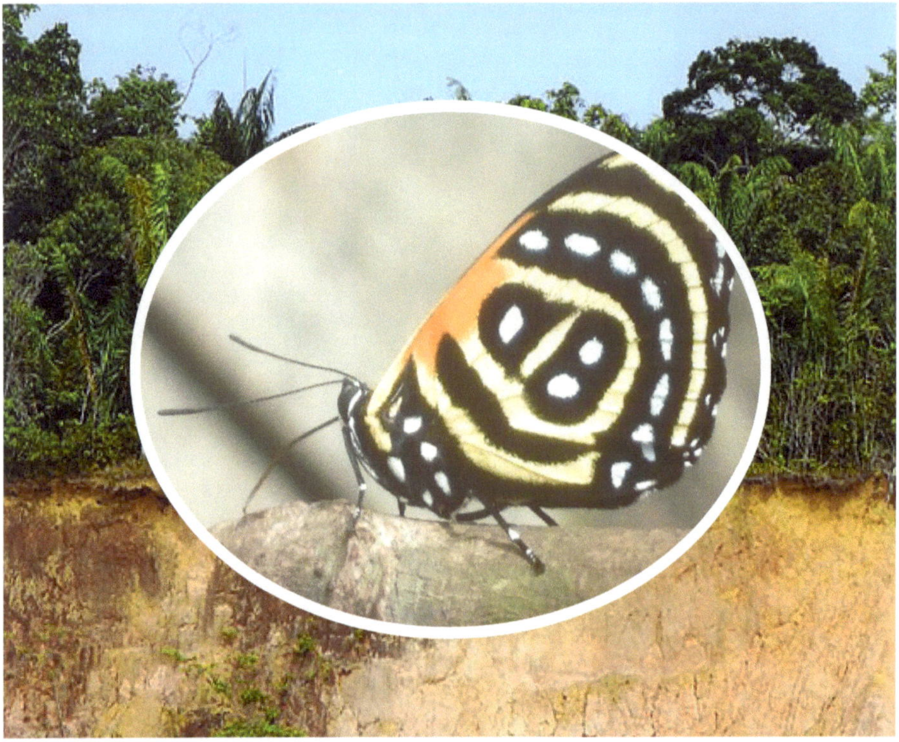

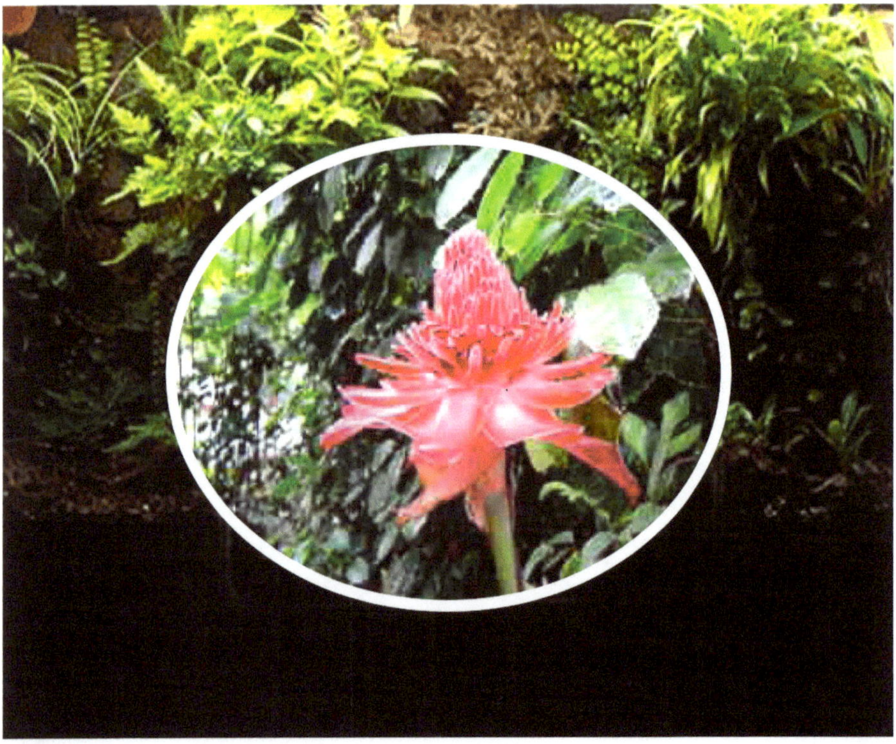

Constantine Issighos   The Amazon Exploration Series

THE AMAZON ETHNOBOTANICAL GARDEN

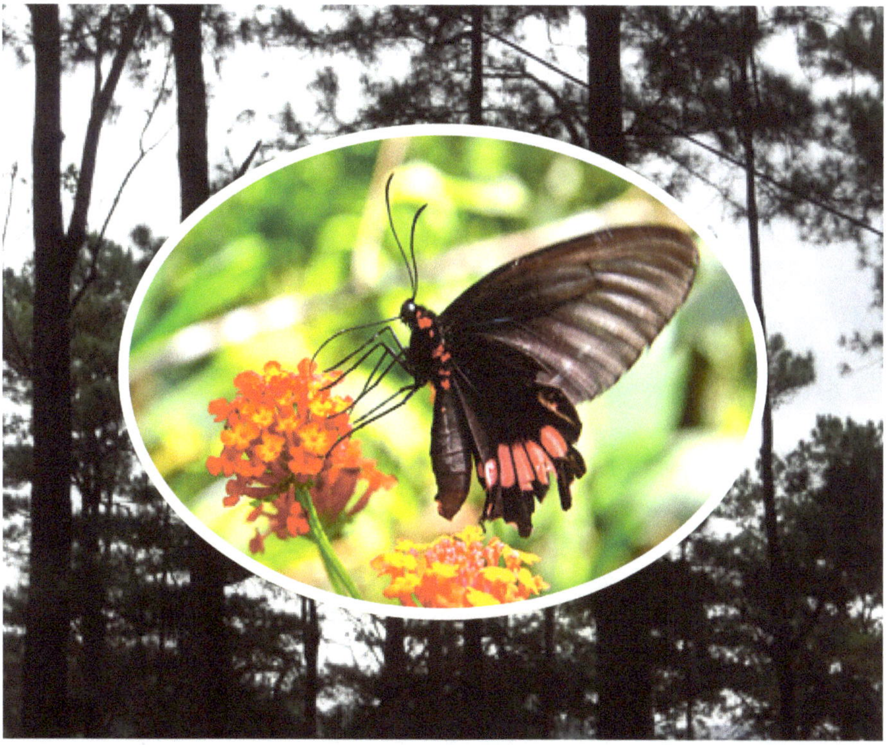

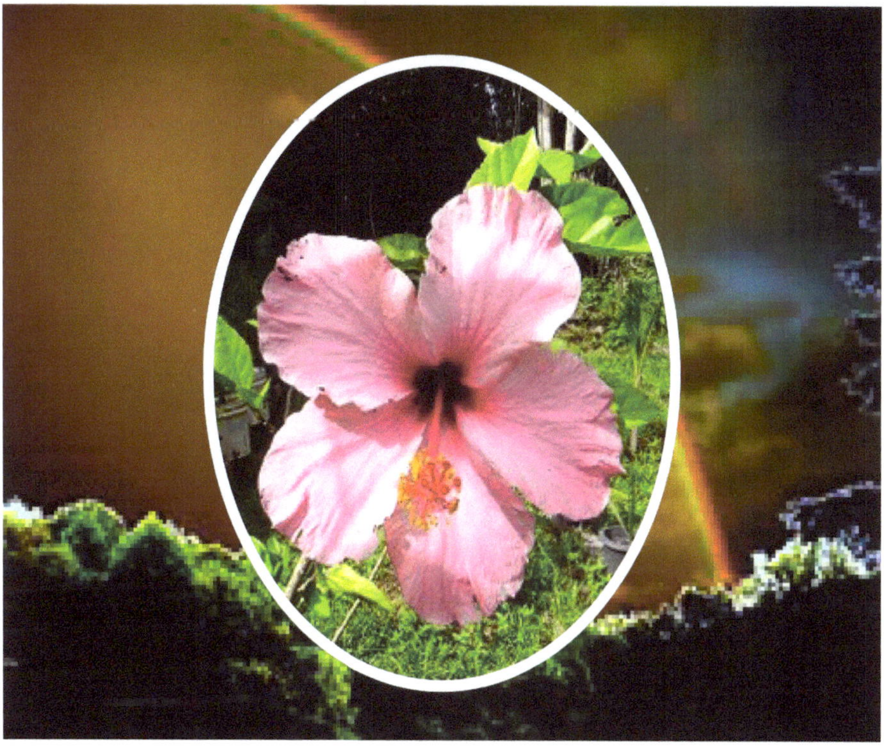

The Amazon Exploration Series	Constantine Issighos

THE AMAZON ETHNOBOTANICAL GARDEN	42

The Amazon Exploration Series   Constantine Issighos

THE AMAZON ETHNOBOTANICAL GARDEN   44

Constantine Issighos The Amazon Exploration Series

THE AMAZON ETHNOBOTANICAL GARDEN

Constantine Issighos　　　　　　The Amazon Exploration Series

THE AMAZON ETHNOBOTANICAL GARDEN

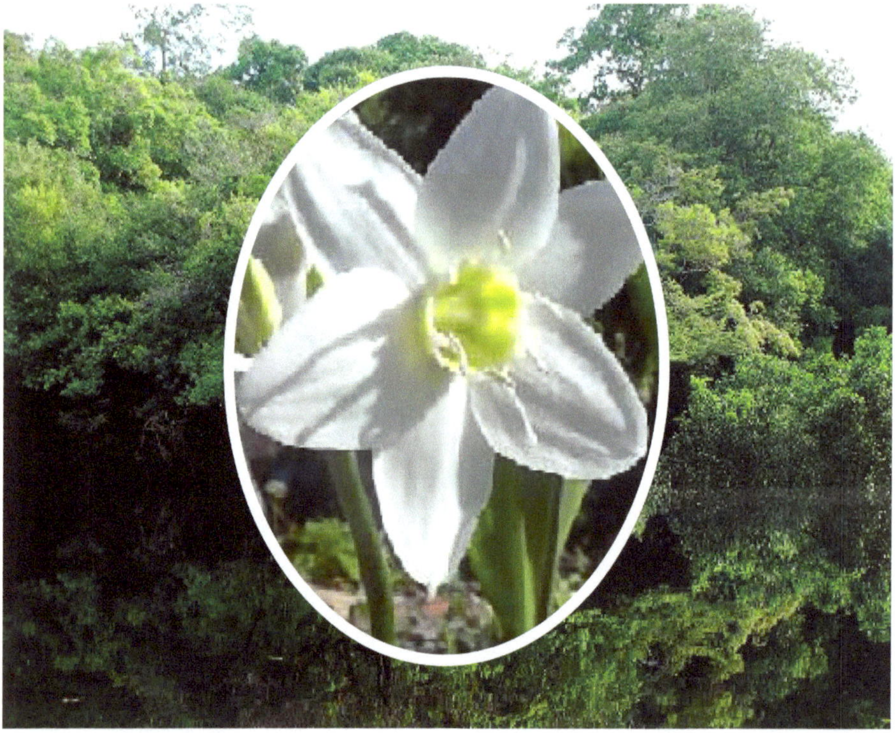

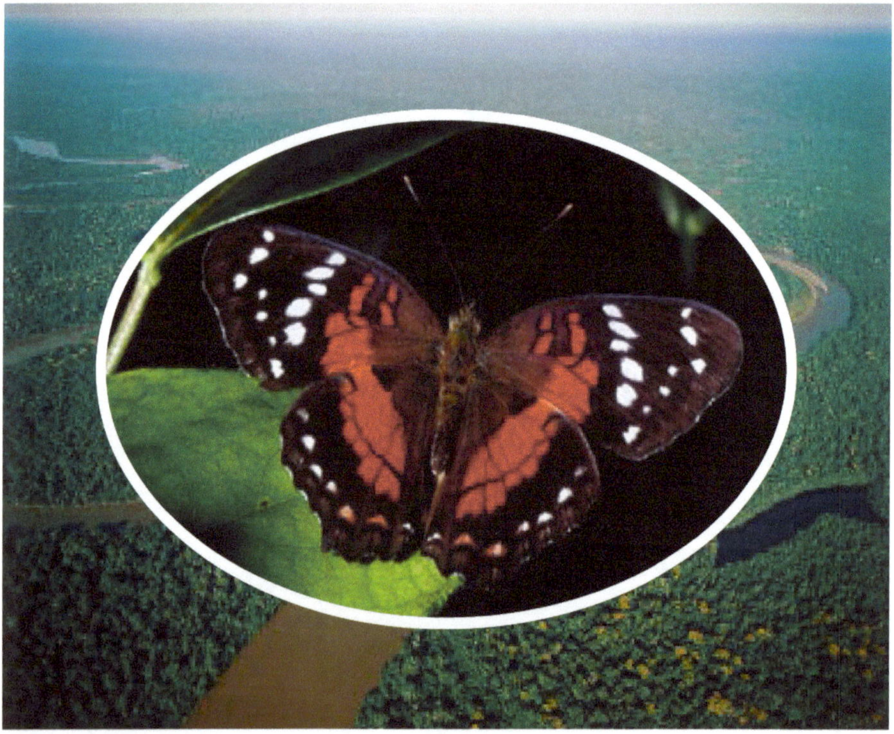

www.ingramcontent.com/pod-product-compliance
Lightning Source LLC
Chambersburg PA
CBHW041754040426
42446CB00001B/24